Dear Parent:

Congratulations! Your child is taking the first steps on an exciting journey. The destination? Independent reading!

STEP INTO READING® will help your child get there. The program offers five steps to reading success. Each step includes fun stories and colorful art. There are also Step into Reading Sticker Books, Step into Reading Math Readers, Step into Reading Phonics Readers, Step into Reading Write-In Readers, and Step into Reading Phonics Boxed Sets—a complete literacy program with something to interest every child.

Learning to Read, Step by Step!

Ready to Read   Preschool–Kindergarten
• big type and easy words • rhyme and rhythm • picture clues
For children who know the alphabet and are eager to begin reading.

Reading with Help   Preschool–Grade 1
• basic vocabulary • short sentences • simple stories
For children who recognize familiar words and sound out new words with help.

Reading on Your Own   Grades 1–3
• engaging characters • easy-to-follow plots • popular topics
For children who are ready to read on their own.

Reading Paragraphs   Grades 2–3
• challenging vocabulary • short paragraphs • exciting stories
For newly independent readers who read simple sentences with confidence.

Ready for Chapters   Grades 2–4
• chapters • longer paragraphs • full-color art
For children who want to take the plunge into chapter books but still like colorful pictures.

STEP INTO READING® is designed to give every child a successful reading experience. The grade levels are only guides. Children can progress through the steps at their own speed, developing confidence in their reading, no matter what their grade.

Remember, a lifetime love of reading starts with a single step!

For Ray Arps
—M.L.

Step into Reading, Random House, and the Random House colophon are registered trademarks of Random House, Inc.

Visit us on the Web!
www.stepintoreading.com
www.randomhouse.com/kids
Educators and librarians, for a variety of teaching tools, visit us at
www.randomhouse.com/teachers

Library of Congress Cataloging-in-Publication Data
Lagonegro, Melissa.
The spooky sound / by Melissa Lagonegro ; illustrated by Ron Cohee.
p. cm. — (Step into reading. Step 2 book)
ISBN 978-0-7364-2664-0 (trade) — ISBN 978-0-7364-8079-6 (lib. bdg.)
I. Cohee, Ron. II. Cars (Motion picture) III. Title.
PZ7.L14317Sp 2010 [E]—dc22 2009023863

Printed in the United States of America   10 9

DISNEY · PIXAR

The
Spooky Sound

By Melissa Lagonegro

Illustrated by Ron Cohee

Random House 🏠 New York

Lightning McQueen and Mater like to tell spooky stories.

Their friends are scared!
But Mater and Lightning
are not.

Lightning and Mater
drive home.
Ahhhoo!
They hear
a spooky sound.

They want
to find out
what it is.

Lightning and
Mater drive by
Ramone's paint shop.
Ahhhoo!

Mater sees

a scary shape.

Is it a monster?

Lightning goes
into the shop.

He finds paint cans!

He tells Mater

there is no monster.

They drive
by Doc's shop.
It is open late.
Ahhhoo!

The sound is louder.
They see
sparks and flames.
Is it a fire monster?

Mater is scared.
But there is
no fire monster.
Doc is fixing Sarge.

The cars drive
to Casa Della Tires.
Ahhhoo!
The sound is closer.
Mater sees
a creepy shape.

Is it a monster
with two heads?

Lightning finds
tall piles of tires.
Luigi and Guido
are having a sale.

Mater and Lightning
drive into the desert.

Ahhhoo!

Mater sees a light
in the sky.
Is it a monster
that glows?

Lightning spots
Al Oft.
He is taking
a night flight.

Lightning and Mater keep driving.

<u>Ahhhoo!</u>

The sound is right behind them!

Mater is really scared!

Lightning wants
to find the sound.
He turns around
very slowly.

The spooky sound
is not a monster!
It does not have fire.
It does not have
two heads.

It does not glow.

It is Sheriff!

He is driving

in his sleep!

Lightning and Mater
laugh and laugh.
They are
not afraid!

But then they see
two glowing eyes!
Oh, no!
What is it?

They do not want
to find out!

S is for Sleeping Bear Dunes

A National Lakeshore Alphabet

Written by Kathy-jo Wargin • Illustrated by Gijsbert van Frankenhuyzen

A a

A is for Arrowhead,
 sign of respect,
 a symbol for all
 and the parks we protect.

Welcome to Sleeping Bear Dunes National Lakeshore!

The Sleeping Bear Dunes National Lakeshore is managed by the National Park Service, a part of the federal government.

In 1962, the arrowhead became the official emblem of the National Park Service (NPS). The outline of the arrowhead represents the history and archaeology of each park, while the elements within the arrowhead are symbols representing the types of features the NPS works hard to protect.

In the arrowhead emblem you will find a sequoia tree, which represents all plants and vegetation; a mountain to symbolize all land formations; a lake that stands for all waters; and a bison signifying all wildlife.

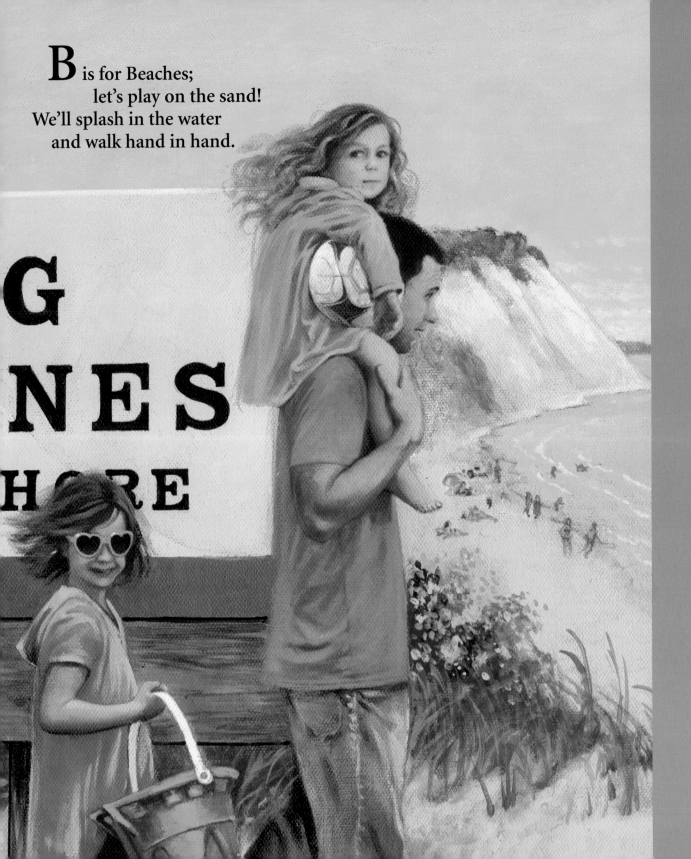

B is for Beaches;
    let's play on the sand!
We'll splash in the water
    and walk hand in hand.

Long, sandy stretches of shoreline make perfect beaches in the Sleeping Bear Dunes area. There are many to choose from, such as the beaches at Glen Haven, North Bar Lake, Peterson Road, the Sleeping Bear Point Maritime Museum, and more.

Swimmers may find Lake Michigan a bit cooler than inland lakes, and because there are no lifeguards on duty, should always be aware of conditions and plan beach-going activities accordingly.

Bb

C is for Cherries,
　　a Michigan treat,
they're perfect to pick,
　　and simple to eat!

What's your favorite cherry treat? Mm, Mm.

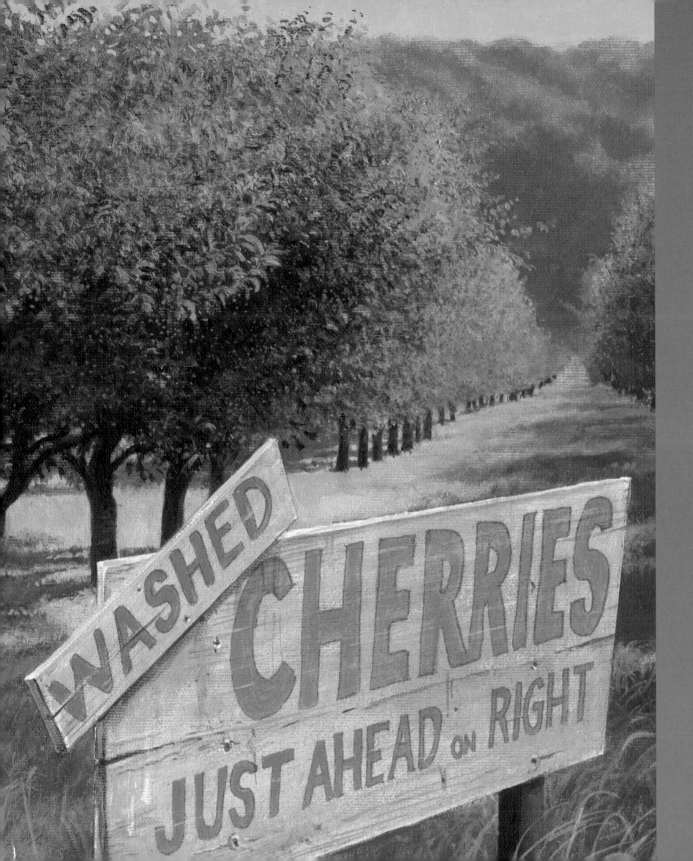

Sandy soil combined with the temperate climate of the eastern portion of Lake Michigan creates a great environment for growing cherries. Michigan is a leader when it comes to cherry production. It grows the majority of tart cherries in the U.S. today, and also contributes approximately 20 percent of the nation's sweet-cherry production. Easy to pick and fun to eat, there are plenty of places to find cherries and cherry products in the Sleeping Bear Dunes area.

From roadside stands to busy shops, cherries are easy to find and enjoy!

The National Cherry Festival is held in Traverse City, Michigan, each year in July. It began as the "Blessing of the Blossoms Festival" in 1925, and over time has evolved into a national celebration.

Cc

The Dune Climb is a tradition and must-do activity for most visitors. The Dune Center is located at the bottom of the Dune Climb, and contains a park store and restrooms. There is also a picnic area so hungry climbers can enjoy a rest and some nourishment.

The hike up the vast, 200-foot sandy hillside is somewhat strenuous, but when you arrive at the top you are rewarded with expansive views of rolling hills and Glen Lake in the distance. When it's time to return down the hill, most visitors will jump or hop, letting gravity assist them along the way. It's important not to descend too quickly and to be aware of sticks or sharp objects in the sand.

Dd

D is for Dune Climb!
Let's run to the top—
we can zip down
with a leap and a hop!

Ready, my friend? Let's do it again!

E is for Empire!
Learn of the past:
the heart of the park
holds the stories that last.

Ee

The village of Empire is the site of the Empire Area Museum Complex as well as the visitor center for the Sleeping Bear Dunes National Lakeshore. The visitor center hosts maps and displays and plenty of helpful volunteers and rangers.

Located in the heart of Sleeping Bear Dunes National Lakeshore, Empire was founded in 1851, but was not incorporated as a village until years later in 1895. It was named for the schooner "Empire," which was stranded there during a winter storm in 1865.

In Leland, Michigan, there remains a collection of docks, shanties, fishing tugs, and smokehouses known as Fishtown. Once part of a thriving commercial fishing trade, today it is one of only a few working fishing villages in Michigan, and now primarily connects visitors to the maritime fishing heritage of Michigan and the Great Lakes.

Though Leland is not specifically within the bounds of the Sleeping Bear Dunes National Lakeshore, the Leland Harbor offers ferry services to the North and South Manitou Islands.

Fis for Fishtown.
    The nets hang to dry
on the docks near the shanties
    as tugs putter by.

G is for Ghost Forest.
Here you will see
the spires in sand
telling tales of each tree.

Barren trunks and tree branches poking up from the sand tell the ecological story of the dunes. Such places where spires appear through the sand are called "ghost forests."

A ghost forest is created when base amounts of sand accumulate, allowing vegetation and trees to grow within. Over the course of decades, more sand, deposited through wind, weather, and time, will move in and bury the trees, suffocating them in layers. Later, when the wind sends the sand once again on its way, barren branches will emerge.

Ghost forests are an important part of the Sleeping Bear Dunes ecology and should not be disturbed.

The farms you will find in the Sleeping Bear Dunes National Lakeshore are an important collection of buildings and locations because unlike most farms today, they have remained free of urban development.

The D. H. Day farm is one that can be spotted from the top of the Dune Climb with its pristine white buildings. The barn and outbuildings were built in the late 1880s and early 1890s. Today the farm is privately owned and is not part of the park's collection.

Though you will find several farms and cabins throughout the park, the Port Oneida Rural Historic District, three miles north of Glen Arbor, is the largest collection in the park and includes settlements that were farmed for over 100 years. The Port Oneida district is a well-preserved area of 3,000 farming acres, and visitors are welcome to linger on these properties.

H is for Homestead.
A house with a stoop,
a barn and a silo,
an old chicken coop.

Ii

I is for Islands—I see them, do you?
  The islands are named North and South Manitou.
Important to shipping a long time ago,
  now campers explore them with backpacks in tow.

The only way to reach North or South Manitou Island is by passenger ferry service or private boat. The islands offer a remote and rustic experience for visitors; there are no food services or stores on either island, but there is emergency medical assistance if needed.

North Manitou Island has a rich history of lumber and farming, and was once the location of a U.S. Life-Saving Service Station. Today few signs of its past remain. Now it is primarily managed as a wilderness, and visitors enjoy backpacking and camping as the only method of travel is by foot. The 100-foot lighthouse tower of South Manitou Island Lighthouse is a familiar landmark. There is also a visitor center and the Valley of the Giants, home to some of the largest white cedars in Michigan.

Jack-in-the-Pulpit
begins with a **J**—
One hood with a pouch;
Did you spot one today?

The jack-in-the-pulpit thrives in the beech-maple forests of Michigan. Blending into their environment of brown and green, this plant lives up to its name with one to two large glossy leaves and a separate stalk that features a large hooded flower that is green with brownish stripes.

Plants and wildflowers thrive in the Sleeping Bear Dunes National Lakeshore because of the diverse weather and habitats. Plants that thrive in hot sandy conditions include searocket and bearberry, while flowers of the forest include trout lily, trailing arbutus, and bloodroot as well as pink, yellow, and showy lady's slippers. The marshes of the park have their own flora; marsh marigolds are common and in the sandy dunes, beach pea and blue harebells make many appearances.

Jj

The rivers and streams of Sleeping Bear Dunes National Lakeshore are a floater's paradise. The two major rivers, the Platte River and the Crystal River, are popular kayak, canoe, and inner-tube destinations.

The Platte River, located in the southern portion of the park, is shallow, clear, and slow moving, and with no rapids or tumult, has become a favored recreational spot for people of all ages.

The Crystal River is in the northern portion of the park and flows from Glen Lake to Lake Michigan in a slow and winding path. Both rivers provide opportunities to spot wildlife and a variety of plant species as well as fish, frogs, turtles, mayflies, and waterfowl.

K k

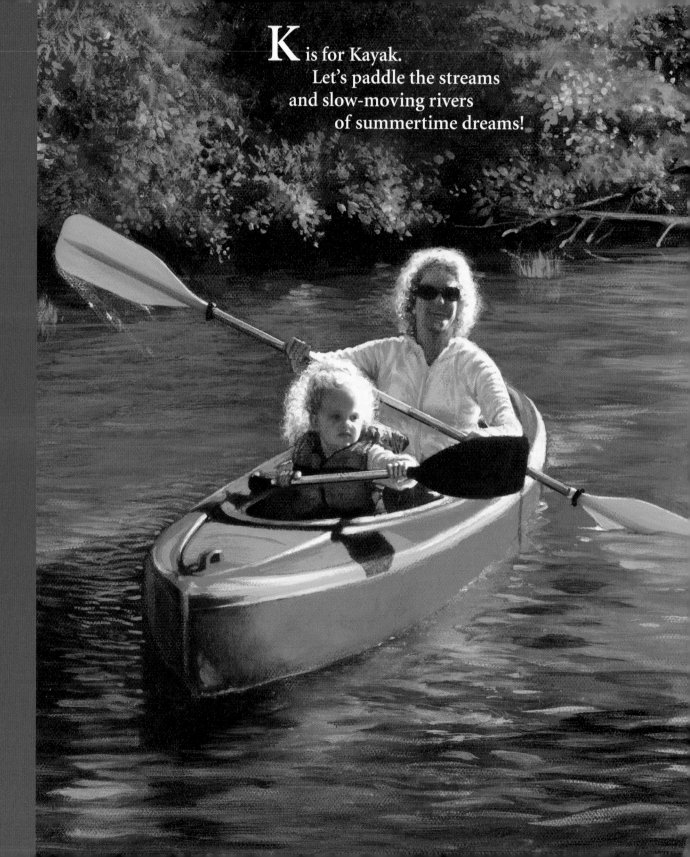

K is for Kayak.
Let's paddle the streams
and slow-moving rivers
of summertime dreams!

L₁

L is Lake Michigan!
Freshwater sea—
we'll ride the waves
as they roll … 1-2-3!

Splish! Splash!

Lake Michigan is the only Great Lake that is located entirely within the United States. The second largest of the five Great Lakes by volume, Lake Michigan is third in size by measure of surface area.

The coastal area of the eastern- and southernmost portion of Lake Michigan is primarily sand, and the eastern shore of the lake consists of the largest freshwater dune system in the world. The Sleeping Bear Dunes National Lakeshore, along with several other parks and forests along the shoreline, contribute to this honor.

Lake Michigan offers many sporting activities such as windsurfing, kayaking, stand-up paddleboarding, and sailing as well as swimming, wading, and splashing in the shallows.

Just west of Glen Haven is the Sleeping Bear Point Coast Guard Station Maritime Museum, where visitors learn about the U.S. Coast Guard, the Life-Saving Service, and the history of Great Lakes shipping. One popular re-enactment is the firing of a Lyle gun, which was once used to fire a rescue line from shore to ships in distress.

The Manitou Passage is a channel between the Manitou Islands and the mainland, and long ago it served as a busy shipping lane. There were frequent shipwrecks, and the skills of those who manned the life-saving stations on both the island and the shore, primarily volunteers, were important to the local communities. The museum is the original Sleeping Bear Point Life-Saving Station, which was moved one mile west to its current location in 1931 due to encroaching sand dunes.

M
m

M is for Maritime.
Heroes are brave,
each lends a hand
with a mission to save.

N is for Night Sky.
When evening turns dark,
the galaxies glimmer
throughout the whole park.

Twinkle, twinkle, little stars.
When it's dark—can you see Mars?

N
n

An unpolluted night sky is important to the future legacy of the Sleeping Bear Dunes National Lakeshore. The National Park Service is committed to preserving the chance for all to see the stars of a night sky and the Sleeping Bear Dunes is one of the last places where total darkness can be experienced.

The park presents night-sky programs at various locations of the park so visitors can learn about stars and stargazing, planets, eclipses, meteor showers, galaxies, and more.

Pierce Stocking was a Michigan lumberman who loved the nature of the bluffs towering above Lake Michigan. Inspired by the beauty of the land south of Glen Haven that he had purchased from D. H. Day, he grew to have a desire to share it with others. To do so, he imagined a road that would reach the top of the dunes. In 1967, seven years after initial planning began, this road opened to the public as the Sleeping Bear Dunes Park.

Pierce Stocking operated the scenic drive until he passed away in 1976. In 1977 the road became part of the Sleeping Bear Dunes National Lakeshore and, eventually, was renamed for the man who first envisioned it.

O o

O is for Overlook.
Stop and explore
the wide scenic vistas
from bluffs to the shore.

Oh, what a view!

P p

The piping plover (*Charadrius melodus*) is an endangered species due to loss of habitat and predation. This shorebird nests only on beaches and requires long expanses of quiet nesting area. There are only three small populations, one of which is here in the Great Lakes. There are between 50 and 60 nesting pairs in the entire Great Lakes area, with the largest concentration of those birds existing in the Sleeping Bear Dunes area. The piping plover makes a sweet whistle that sounds like "peep-lo."

An exceptional place to spot birds is the Sleeping Bear Birding Trail, which includes a flyway and thousands of acres along Lake Michigan. This trail is primarily undisturbed, therefore making it a fine habitat for the endangered piping plover.

P is for Piping Plover;
let's do our best
to save shoreline places so
pairs safely nest.

When winter descends upon the park, a quiet and tranquil mood allows visitors to see the park through a unique perspective. The hills are covered with snow, which mutes the sounds of busier seasons.

There are many ways to explore the park in the quietest days of winter. Snowshoeing is permitted on all the snow-covered dunes, fields, and forest areas of the park. The park does offer guided snowshoe hikes and these ranger-led activities allow a chance to look for signs of wildlife and learn new facts about the lakeshore.

Cross-country skiing is also a popular activity, as most of the hiking trails become covered in snow. Sledding is another winter activity, and permitted at the Dune Climb in a designated area. There is also winter camping and ice fishing.

Q is for Quiet.
When winter prevails,
there's ice on the lakes,
and snow on the trails.

The ranger is an important figure to the conservation, preservation, and education of the park's resources. With a duty and responsibility to uphold the rules of the park and share them with others, to set and enforce policy, and to help visitors understand and enjoy the unique features of each park, a ranger's duties may be as diverse as the park he or she serves. In the Sleeping Bear Dunes National Lakeshore, rangers lead programs, oversee safety concerns, engage with visitors, and play an important role in protecting the cultural integrity of the park so that future generations may enjoy the same landscape and opportunities it provides.

At the Sleeping Bear Dunes National Lakeshore, there is also the opportunity for children to become Junior Rangers.

R r

R is for Ranger.
It's their special duty
to share with the world
all of nature's fine beauty.

S s

The park's namesake is from a legend passed down through the generations. In the story, a mother bear and her cubs flee a Wisconsin forest fire. The cubs vanish as they swim across Lake Michigan, and when Mother Bear reaches the shore, she climbs atop the highest hill to watch for their return. She waits so long that she falls asleep in her sorrow. Years pass, and the cubs emerge from the water as two islands to reward her for her patience.

Today the Sleeping Bear Dune can be viewed from the Sleeping Bear Dune Overlook. The dune was once approximately 234 feet high and much larger and darker in appearance with its dense vegetation cover. Due to erosion and wave action, it has been steadily decreasing in size.

S is for Sleeping Bear—
Sands gently sweep,
    where mother bear waits
and has fallen asleep.

T is for Trails!
It's time for a hike.
The paths stretch for miles;
we can run, walk, or bike.

Tt

There are more than 100 miles of designated hiking trails in the Sleeping Bear Dunes National Lakeshore, which include 13 trails in the main area of the park, and additional trails on both islands. While the trails that flow through diverse ecosystems are to be used primarily for hiking, many are maintained for winter activities as well.

The recently developed and still-in-progress Sleeping Bear Heritage Trail, which is managed by the Friends of Sleeping Bear Dunes, is a paved, multiuse, non-motorized trail that will span 27 miles when complete. As the first trail to allow bicycles because it is paved, it offers a wide array of recreational opportunities such as biking, rollerblading, and strolling.

U u

"Up North" is a popular yet casual term to describe the spirit of the woods, lakes, and locations of northern Michigan. It's most often heard as a fond Michigan colloquialism. "Where are you going this weekend?" The answer: "Up North."

Up North starts with U!
It's our way to say,
we're getting outdoors
to explore and to play!

V is for Vacation.
        Pitch the tent; let's have a s'more.
We'll sing happy campfire songs,
        tell stories, jokes, and more.

What's your favorite campfire story?

Camping is a popular activity in the Sleeping Bear Dunes. There are several campgrounds such as the Platte River Campground, the D. H. Day Campground, and group campgrounds. There is also an opportunity for backcountry camping on North and South Manitou Islands, which are accessible by ferry.

V
v

Wildlife is abundant in the Sleeping Bear Dunes National Lakeshore, most in part due to the diverse ecology and habitat it provides. Though the park may include one famous sleeping bear in the shape of a dune, live black bears are rarely spotted in the area. Most commonly seen are river otters, coyotes, raccoons, striped skunks, eastern cottontails, beavers, white-footed mice, eastern chipmunks, and red squirrels. In addition to the many birds, common amphibians and reptiles include eastern American toads, northern spring peepers, and eastern garter snakes.

W is for Wildlife:
fox and white-tailed deer,
raccoon and beaver, porcupine—
you can find them here.

An **X** on our map
for the road near the shore,
twisting and turning,
M-22— let's explore!

Highway M-22 is an iconic and pleasurable road that defines much of the larger Sleeping Bear Dunes area. It travels through the quaint towns of Glen Arbor, Empire, Sutton's Bay, Northport, and more. In all, the drive is 117 miles long and filled with an array of eclectic shops, eateries, and stunning natural views.

Y is for Year—
1970 the mark,
we welcomed the dunes
as a national park.

The Sleeping Bear Dunes National Lakeshore is an area that includes a 35-mile span of eastern Lake Michigan shoreline and more than 71,000 acres of land, as well as the North and South Manitou Islands.

The park was authorized to become a National Lakeshore by Congress in 1970, established as such for its "outstanding natural features, including forests, beaches, dune formations, and ancient glacial phenomena...for the benefit, inspiration, education, recreation, and enjoyment of the public." This designation and further development of the park's assets has helped it become one of our nation's natural treasures and a popular vacation destination, with an average of more than one million visitors per year. Philip A. Hart was a United States senator who worked tirelessly to bring about the legislature that created the Sleeping Bear Dunes National Lakeshore.

In 2011, the park earned the title of "Good Morning America's Most Beautiful Place in America," based on an online voting contest sponsored by *Good Morning America*, the popular morning television show.

Z is for Zs
    as sleep fills the air;
it is now twilight for one special bear.

She will be here, upon the far dune,
    she'll hope as she slumbers that you'll come back soon.

The National Park Service works hard to protect the natural resources of the Sleeping Bear Dunes National Lakeshore. Rangers and volunteers are knowledgeable about the many ways visitors can help them continue to ensure the park remains intact for future generations. When visiting, be mindful of the many ways you can be a good steward and when in doubt, ask a park representative for help.

Let's protect our open spaces
for the younger generation,
and leave to them the treasures
of our fine and splendid nation.

Z z

To all who dream of climbing the highest dunes,
and those who favor the small ones, too.

—Kathy-jo

❧

To all Park Rangers

—Gijsbert (Nick)

ILLUSTRATOR'S ACKNOWLEDGMENTS
Gijsbert van Frankenhuyzen wishes to thank and acknowledge
the following people for their assistance and support.

PARK RANGERS FROM THE SLEEPING BEAR DUNES NATIONAL PARK
Peggy Burman, Katie Fredericks, Laurel Kays, Lauren O'Brien, and Mary Peterson

MODELS
Garrett and Trenton Peacock; Ava and Jake; Kees and Tyler; Lydia, Alison,
Dru and Adam Montri; Mika Angelovici and Miles Geiger

HELP
Veronica Wilkerson Johnson; Crystal River Outfitters – Glen Arbor

Text Copyright © 2015 Kathy-jo Wargin
Illustration Copyright © 2015 Gijsbert van Frankenhuyzen

Sleeping Bear Press
2395 South Huron Parkway, Suite 200
Ann Arbor, MI 48104
www.sleepingbearpress.com

Printed and bound in the United States.

10 9 8 7 6 5 4 3 2 1

Library of Congress Cataloging-in-Publication Data

Wargin, Kathy-jo.
S is for Sleeping Bear Dunes : a national lakeshore alphabet /
written by Kathy-jo Wargin ; illustrated by Gijsbert van Frankenhuyzen.
pages cm
Summary: "Following the alphabet this book uses poetry and expository text to explore
the Sleeping Bear Dunes National Lakeshore, which is located along the northwest coast of
the Lower Peninsula of Michigan. Topics include the park's natural features such as dune
formations, beaches, forests, and cultural attractions" —Provided by publisher.
ISBN 978-1-58536-917-1
1. Sleeping Bear Dunes National Lakeshore (Mich.)—Juvenile literature. 2. Alphabet
books—Juvenile literature. I. Frankenhuyzen, Gijsbert van, illustrator. II. Title.
F572.S8W37 2015
977.4'635—dc23   2014035453